# AARON JAY KERNIS

# BALLAD
## FOR CELLO AND PIANO

ISBN 978-1-4234-4239-4

## Associated Music Publishers, Inc.

DISTRIBUTED BY

HAL•LEONARD®
CORPORATION
7777 W. BLUEMOUND RD. P.O. BOX 13819 MILWAUKEE, WI 53213

## COMPOSER'S NOTE

*Ballad* was composed in late 2004 and is dedicated to the memory of my parents Frank and Mildred Kernis. The piece reflects their fondness for lyrical music, and is lightly colored by the influence of jazz harmonies touched on beneath the cello's arching, elegiac lines.

It was first written for eight cellos, for soloist Maya Beiser, and was subsequently arranged for cello and piano. *Ballad* was premiered by cellist Ariane Lallemand and pianist Evelyne Luest on May 1, 2005 at St. Peter's Episcopal Church in New York City.

Duration: 8 minutes

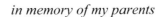

*in memory of my parents*

# BALLAD

AARON JAY KERNIS
2004

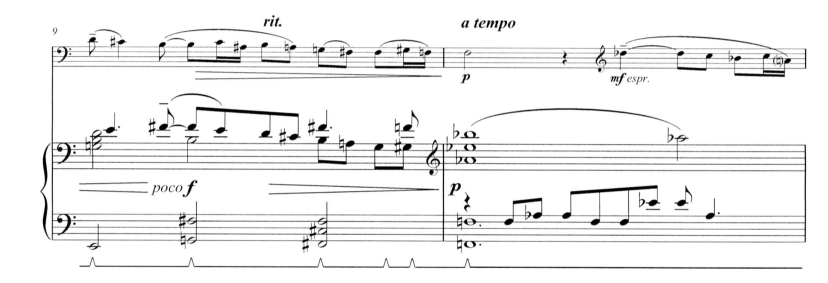

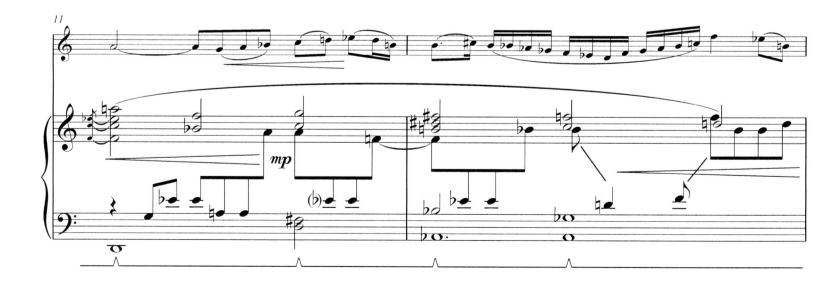

Calmo

allarg.

**With more movement,**
**but still sustained** ♩ = 66

movendo

**Più sostenuto** ♩ = 66

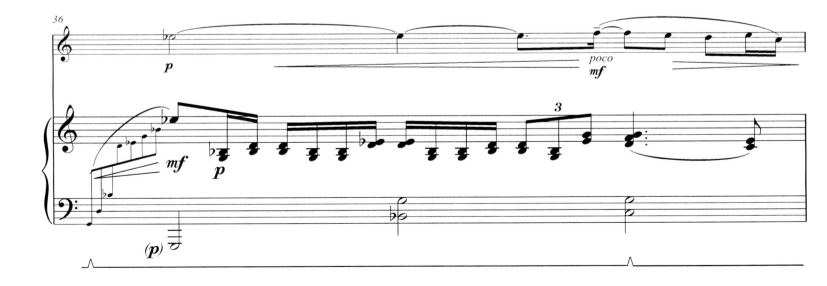

Cello

*in memory of my parents*

# BALLAD

AARON JAY KERNIS
2004

V.S.

Cello

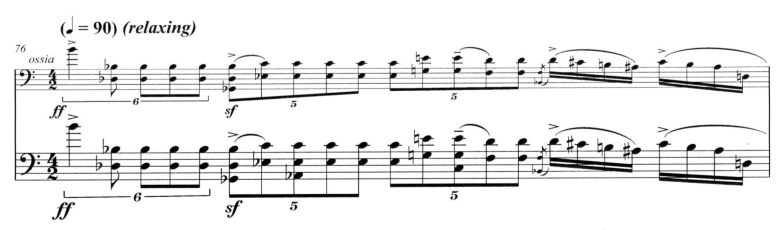

V.S.

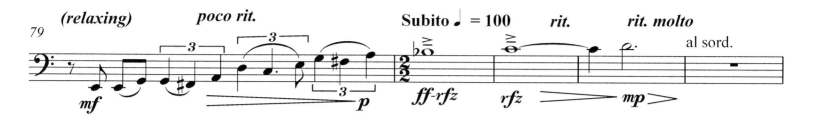

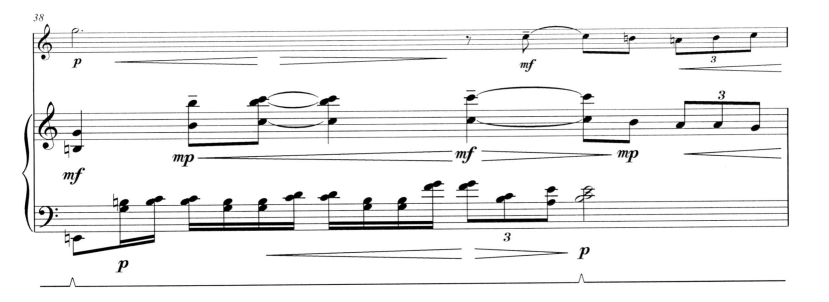

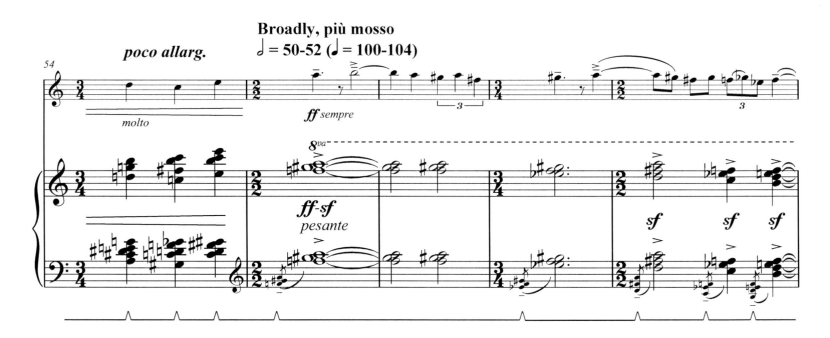

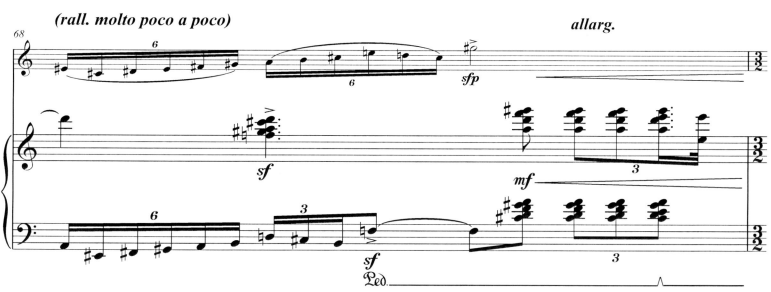

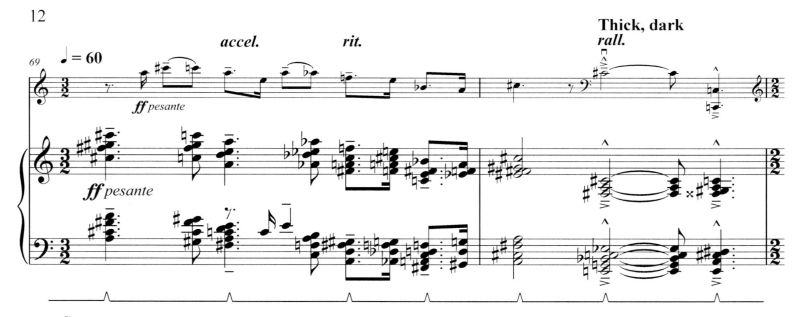

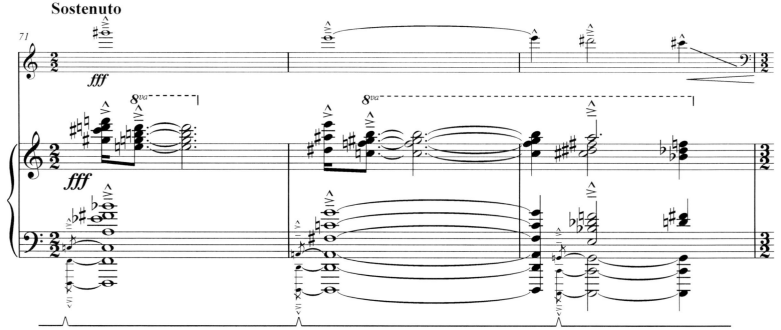

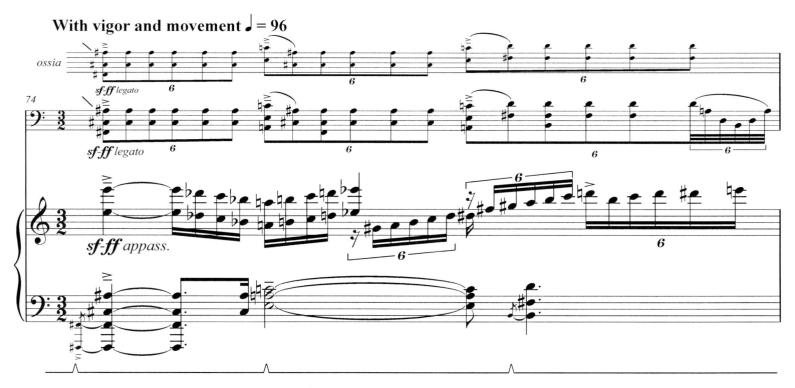

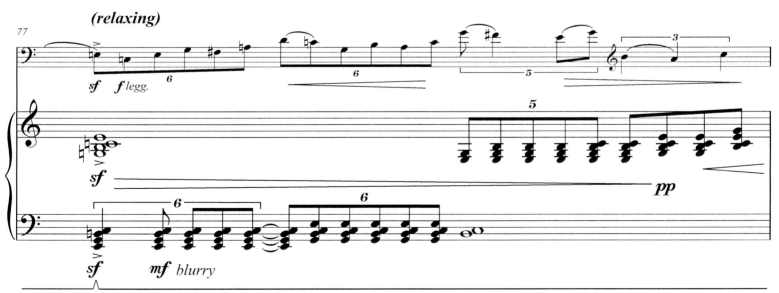

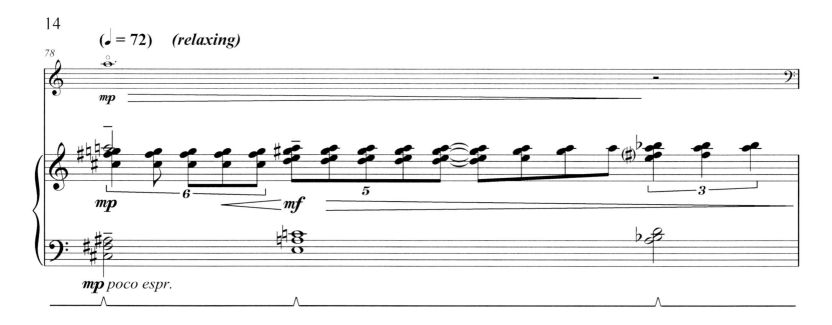

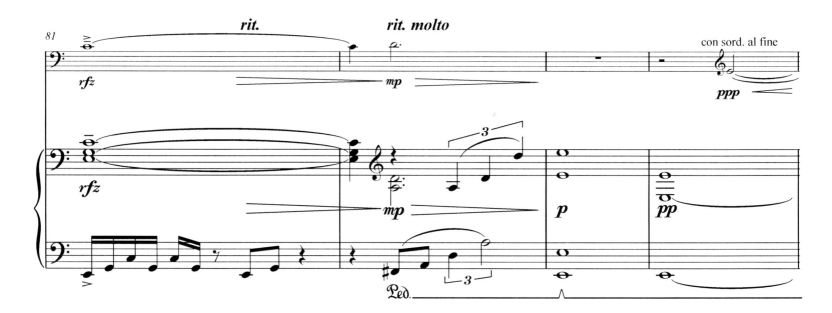

**Adagio** ♩ = 48-52

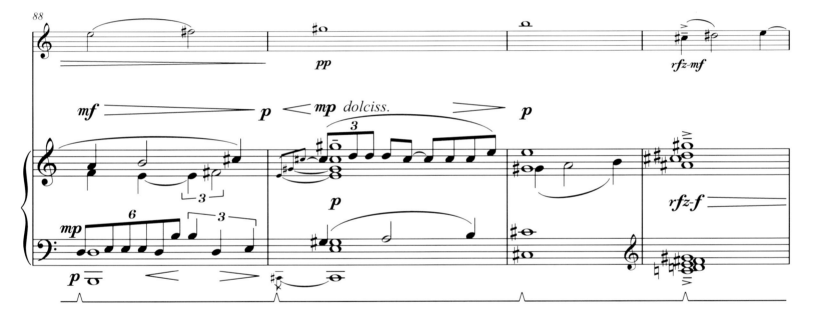